MW00368609

# *Love Songs*
# *A Cappella*

### Contemporary
### A Cappella Songbook

## Love Songs Series
## Volume 1

### *A Cappella Arrangements by*
### *Deke Sharon*

Edited by Anne Raugh

EXCLUSIVELY DISTRIBUTED BY

HAL•LEONARD®
CORPORATION
7777 W. BLUEMOUND RD. P.O. BOX 13819 MILWAUKEE, WI 53213

# Available from Contemporary A Cappella Publishing

## The Contemporary A Cappella Songbook Collection:

*SATB Series*

| | |
|---|---|
| Volume 1 | HL08741649 |
| Volume 2 | HL08741650 |
| Volume 3 – I Feel Good | HL08742598 |
| Volume 4 – Shout! | HL08743512 |

*SSAA Series*

| | |
|---|---|
| Natural Woman | HL08742904 |

*TTBB Series*

| | |
|---|---|
| Volume 1 – Good Ol' A Cappella | HL08743513 |
| Volume 2 – Sh-Boom | HL08743514 |

| | |
|---|---|
| Love Songs A Cappella | HL08743515 |
| Jazz Standards A Cappella | HL08743235 |
| A CASA Christmas | HL08741651 |
| Songs for All Occasions | HL08742050 |
| Continuum: The First Songbook of Sweet Honey in the Rock | HL08742029 |
| The Collegiate A Cappella Arranging Manual | HL08742599 |

Available wherever songbooks are sold, or online at *www.a-cappella.com* and *www.casa.org*.

Part-predominant learning tapes are available directly from Mainely A CAPPELLA for the arrangements in:

Contemporary A Cappella Songbook, SATB Series – Volume 1
Contemporary A Cappella Songbook, SATB Series – Volume 2
A CASA Christmas

Call 1.800.827.2936, email *order@a-cappella.com* or order online at *www.a-cappella.com* and specify Soprano, Alto, Tenor, Bass, or a set of all four.

# TABLE OF CONTENTS

Cover photo: Kate Gooding
© 2002 Contemporary A Cappella Publishing
Photo: Don Gooding

# True Colors

Arranged by
Deke Sharon

Words and Music by
Billy Steinberg and Tom Kelly

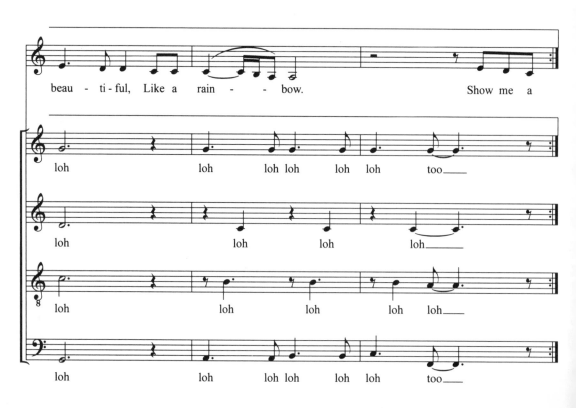

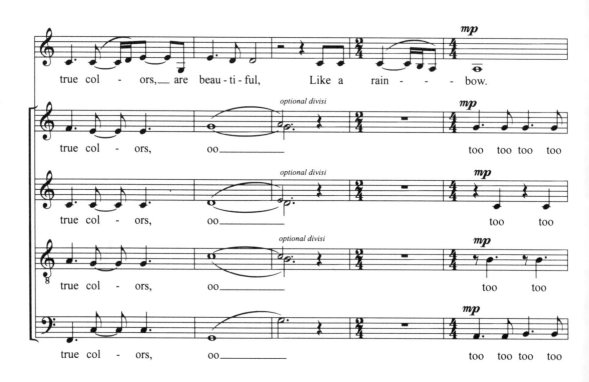

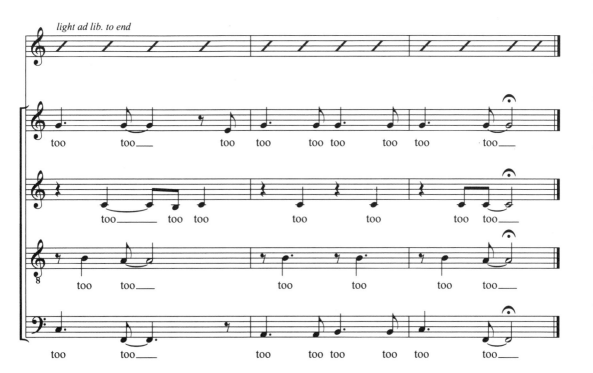

# I Can't Make You Love Me

Arranged by
Deke Sharon

Words and Music by
Mike Reid and Allen Shamblin

10

12

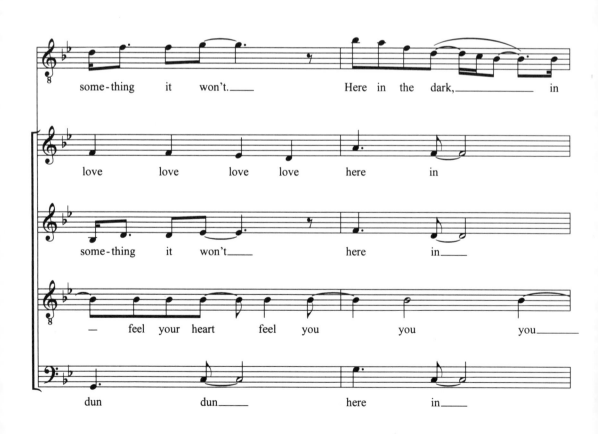

14

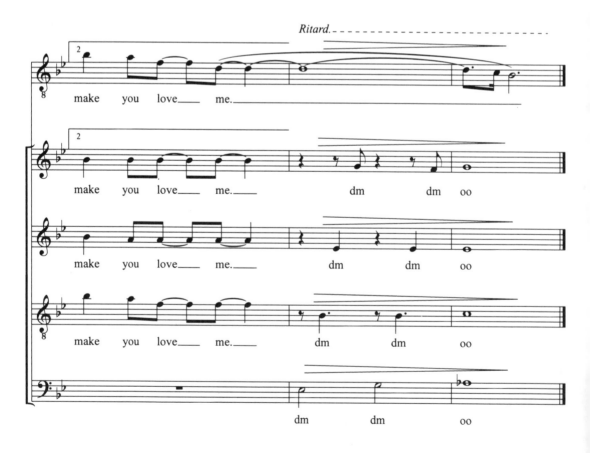

# How Sweet It Is
## (To Be Loved By You)

Arranged by
Deke Sharon

Words and Music by
Edward Holland, Lamont Dozier
and Brian Holland

16

18

20

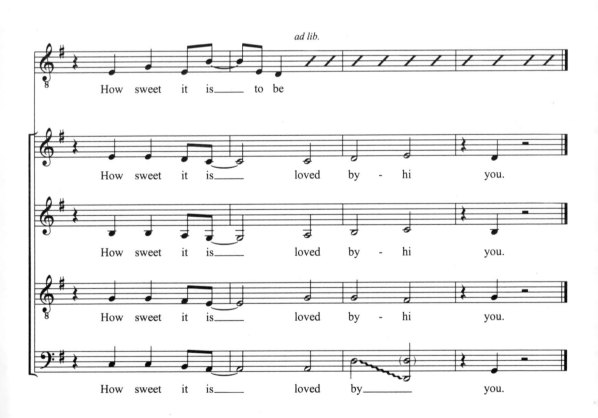

# Helplessly Hoping

Arranged by
Deke Sharon

Written by
Stephen Stills

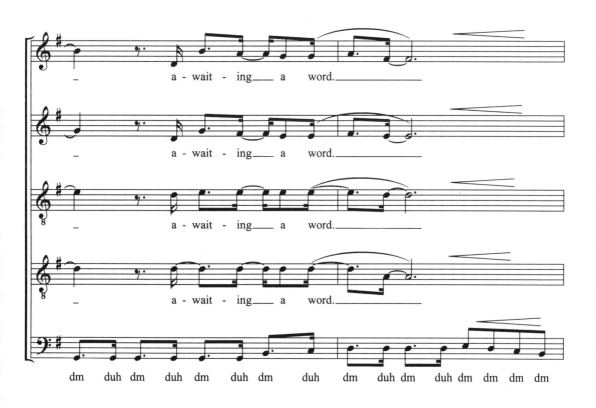

26

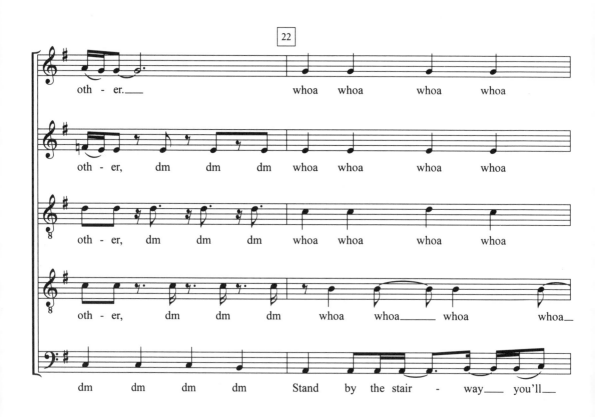

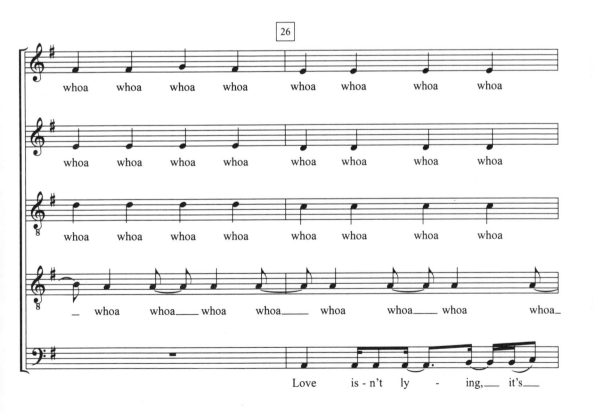

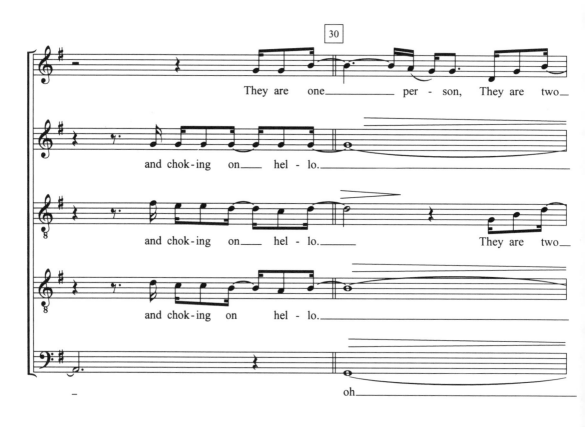

# So Far Away

Arranged by
Deke Sharon

Words and Music by
Carole King

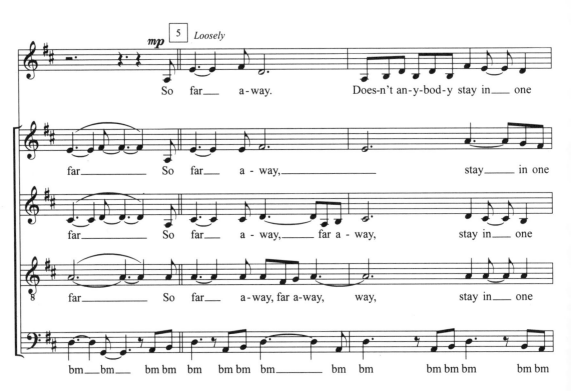

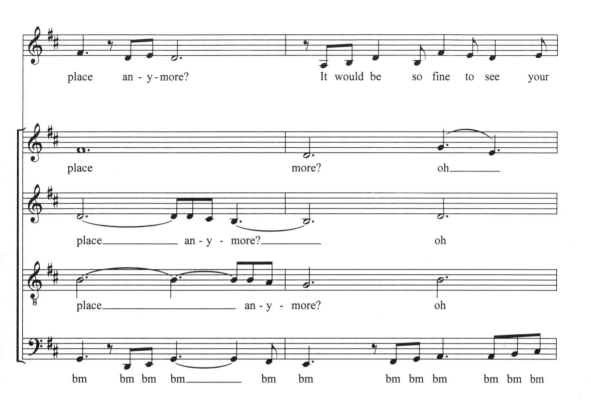

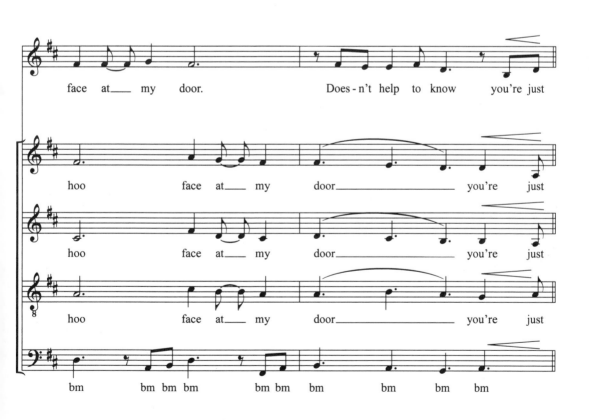

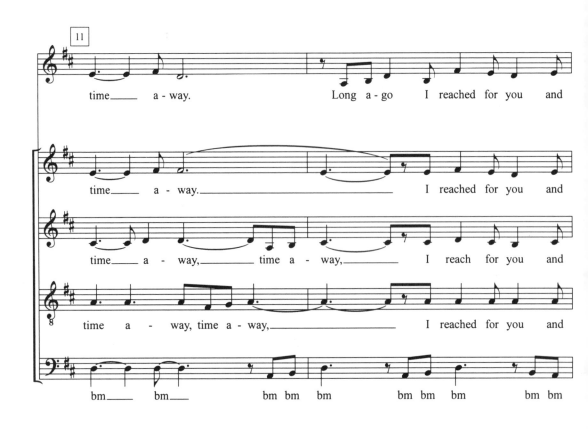

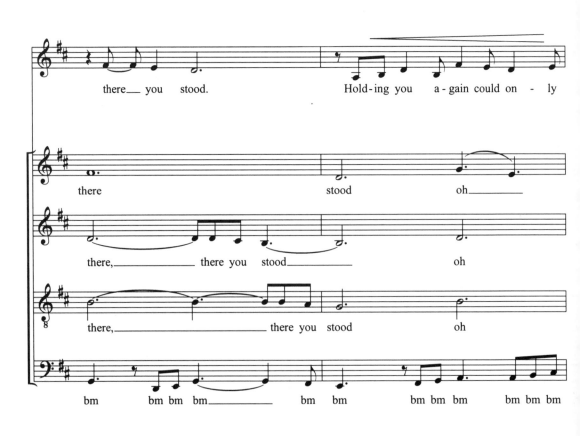

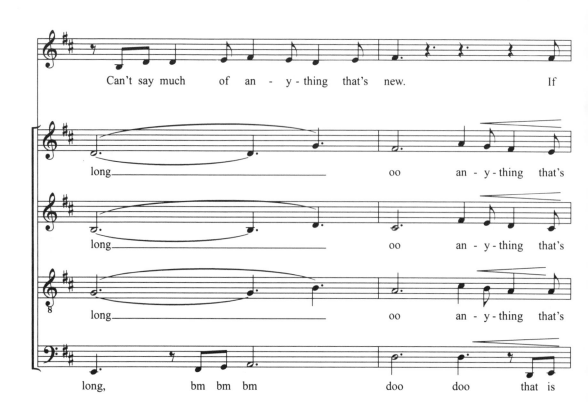

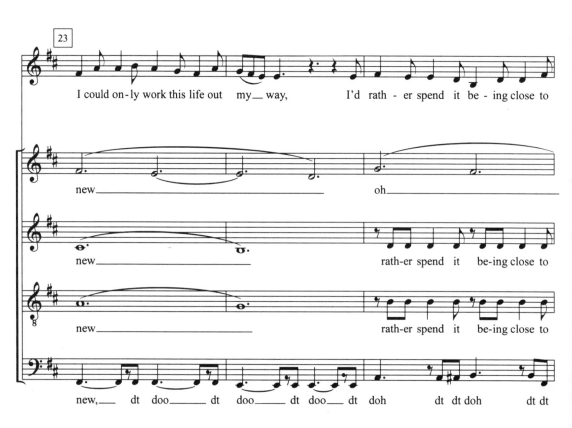

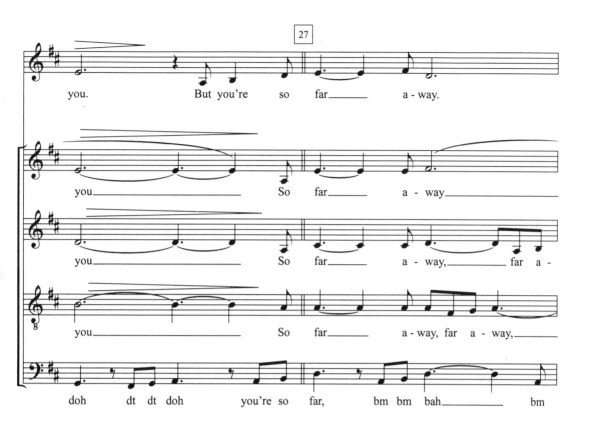

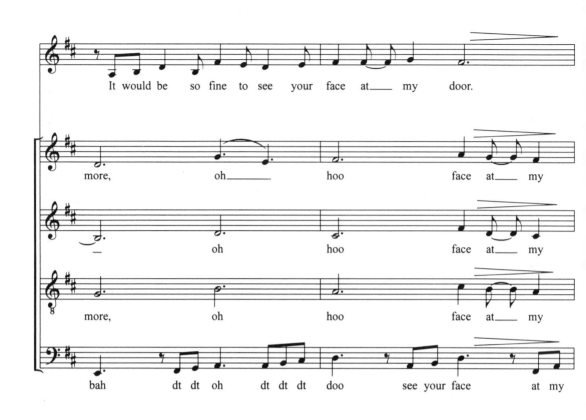

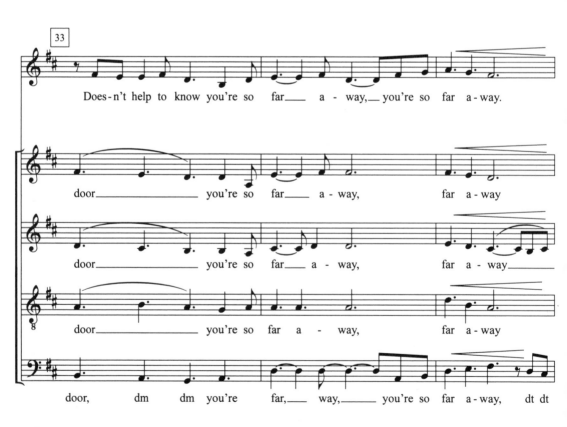

I sure hope the road don't come to own____ me. There's

road_____ don't come to own me

road_____ don't come to own me

road_____ don't come to own me

bm_____ bm bm bm_____ bm bm bm_____ bm bm bm

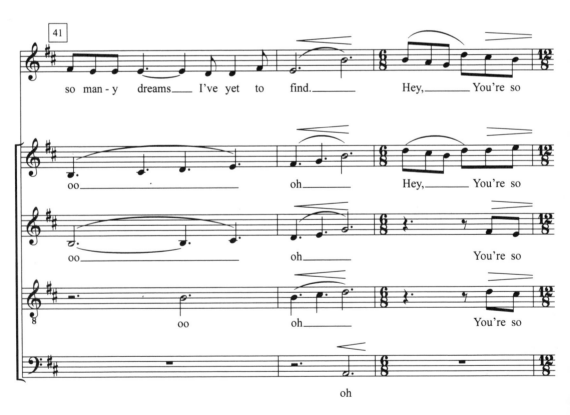

so man-y dreams____ I've yet to find.____ Hey,____ You're so

oo_____ oh____ Hey,____ You're so

oo_____ oh____ You're so

oo oh____ You're so

oh

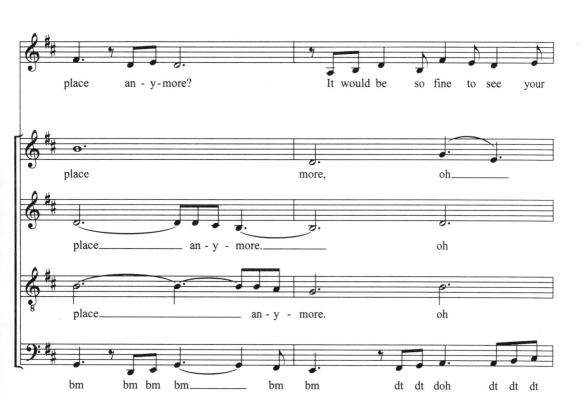

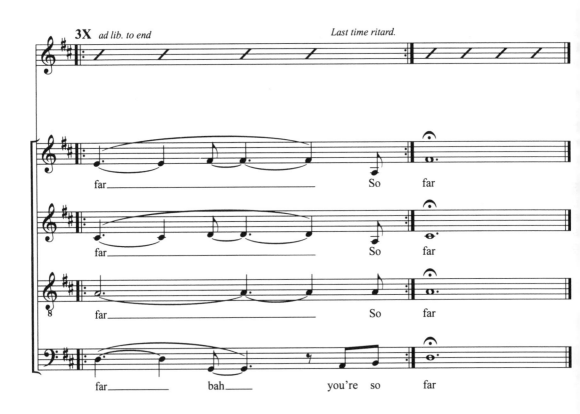

# PERFORMANCE NOTES

When it comes to popular music, traditional Western music notation is, well, inadequate. Use your knowledge of the original songs and internal sense of pop music to turn the black dots on the page into loose, rhythmic rock and roll. This is especially true with solo lines: use the notated solos only as a rough guide (were we to notate the solos exactly as in the originals, they'd often be wildly complex).

Every group is different, and no arrangement can suit them all perfectly, so we encourage you to change our arrangements in any way to better suit your own ensemble.

**True Colors**: Although the overarching effect of the background voices should be smooth, emphasize the *t* of *too* whenever it occurs. The solo can be sung by any voice part (a baritone or a bass with a controlled, light falsetto provides an appropriately pleasing yet vulnerable sound). If you're singing with a large group, consider splitting the solo up between four different people, divided into Verse 1, Chorus 1, Verse 2, and Chorus 2 through the end.

**I Can't Make You Love Me**: This version of Bonnie Raitt's aching ballad should be sung as slowly as can be maintained without sluggishness, allowing each chord to ring. If your group's tuning is good, allow color notes and dissonances to remain just as loud as major chord tones. Combined, the slow tempo and dissonances will underscore the soloist's desire to linger in this uneasy moment.

**How Sweet It Is**: Based primarily on the James Taylor recording (on his "Greatest Hits"), this arrangement should be sung with a bouncy swing feel and lots of playfulness, especially in the background voices. The solo is free to sing *ad lib.* in any spaces and alter the melody freely in the verses.

**Helplessly Hoping**: Make sure the arpeggiated 16th notes at measure 17 are clean and balanced. When correct, the effect is like a plucked acoustic guitar. At measure 22, if you're having trouble keeping your singer's diphthongs together, consider singing *oh* on the first half of each note and *oo* on the second half. If you have more than one person singing each part, consider having just a quartet sing the first six measures.

**So Far Away**: Although not often emphasized in the parts, a strong 2 & 4 are essential to keeping the song moving. Snapping on 2 & 4 works well to keep this momentum. Make sure your singers are comfortable with all the major 7ths, as they're a large part of the harmony. This version is on the House Jacks' live album "Drive," and is often performed as their final encore, without microphones.

## The Contemporary A Cappella Society
*is a non-profit organization formed in 1990 to foster and promote a cappella music. We serve both the fan and the performer.*

# Membership Levels

**BASIC:** For only $35 a year ($25 with student ID; $40 outside the U.S.), basic membership includes a subscription to the Contemporary A Cappella News (CAN). The CAN is a bi-monthly newsletter that includes international news and concert calendars, guest columns by big names in the a cappella industry, interviews with top groups, how-to articles and album reviews.

**PREMIUM:** For those in a group or serious about a cappella, premium membership at $50 a year ($35 with student ID; $55 outside the U.S.) includes the benefits of basic membership plus: one free classified ad in the CAN; the A Cappella Directory; discounts on custom arrangements from the Ultimate A Cappella Arranging Service; discounts on recordings and songbooks from Mainely A Cappella; and discounts on other a cappella-related merchandise and services, including album production. As an added benefit, if one member of a group joins at the Premium level, other members of the group may receive additional copies of the CAN for just $10 a year (each).

**SPONSOR:** For $100 a year ($110 outside the U.S.), Sponsors enjoy all the benefits of premium membership plus a custom-pressed CD copy of each A Cappella Radio International (ARI) monthly broadcast, and one complementary copy of a CASA publication (such as *Starting an A Cappella Group*).

**BENEFACTOR:** For $250 a year, Benefactors enjoy all the benefits of Sponsors plus: one hot-off-the-press copy of the annual *Best of College A Cappella (BOCA)* CD; the annual *Contemporary A Cappella Recording Awards (CARA)* CD; and one complementary copy of any CASA-produced CD.

**PATRON:** For $500 a year, Patrons enjoy all of the above plus special VIP benefits throughout the year, including access to private, CASA-sponsored concerts.

# CASA Productions

- The **Urban Harmony Movement**, a free community enhancing singing programs for teens and adults
- The **A Cappella Summit**, which brings hundreds of fans, performers and enthusiasts together for two days of seminars, concerts and workshops
- The **Contemporary A Cappella Recording Awards**, a yearly quest for the best recorded a cappella music from around the globe
- **A Cappella Community Awards**, allowing fans to vote for their favorite groups
- The **A Cappella Summit**, which brings hundreds of fans, performers and enthusiasts together for two days of seminars, concerts and workshops
- The **Northern Harmony** Canadian a cappella festival and competition
- The **International Championship of Collegiate A Cappella**, a competition involving college groups of all styles from across North America
- The **A Cappella Almanac**, the complete a cappella website with links to all CASA programs and everything else you might want to know about a cappella
- The **International A Cappella Recording Archives**, a library of over 3,000 a cappella recordings

- **A Cappella Radio International**, a monthly program of news and interviews, broadcast internationally and on the World Wide Web
- **Contemporary A Cappella Recording Awards CD**, including the best submissions from nominees and winners
- The **Urban Harmony Movement R&B CD**, featuring professional and collegiate groups
- The **Northern Harmony CD**, featuring performances from the inaugural year of that festival
- The **Best of College A Cappella (BOCA) CD** series, produced jointly with Mainely A Cappella
- **Class Notes: The Best of Highschool A Cappella CD**, a compilation of outstanding highschool groups
- The **Definitive A Cappella Press Kit**, a guide for groups putting together their own promotional material
- **Producing the Ultimate A Cappella Show**, a how-to manual covering everything from single-group concerts to festivals
- **Starting an A Cappella Group**, a basic guide to starting up your own group for fun or profit

**TO JOIN**, send a check to:

**CASA**
**PMB 1449**
**1850 Union Street #4**
**San Francisco, CA  94123**
**USA**

For more information, drop us a line:

**Phone: 1.415.563.5224**
**Fax: 1.415.921.2834**
**Email: casa@casa.org**
**World Wide Web: http://www.casa.org/**

# Other A Cappella Resources

**MAINELY A CAPPELLA (MAC)**
MAC is a mail-order catalog published annually with quarterly updates. It features more than 2,000 titles, including rare and international releases. The catalog represents a wide range of styles and genres - from the latest in pop, jazz and world bands to classical ensembles and barbershop harmonies.

**MAC Yak**
Mainely A CAPPELLA'S electronic newsletter features new releases, pre-releases, and is the only place to find great sale items.

**VARSITY VOCALS**
Varsity Vocals is a student a cappella outreach organization that sponsors five great programs:

The *Best of College A Cappella (BOCA)* annual compilation CD encourages college groups to compete for a place on this sought-after CD.

The *International Championship of Collegiate A Cappella (ICCA)* brings together hundreds of college a cappella singers who compete in regional concerts across North America for a place in the national finals, held in the Avery Fisher Hall of Lincoln Center, New York City.

The *Best of High School A Cappella (BOHSA)* compilation CD features high school groups from all over the world.

*Worldwide A Cappella Music Month (WAMM)* supports the Music Educator's National Conference *Music in Our Schools Month* during March.

The *Vocal Challenge (VC)* brings the musical expertise of professional a cappella groups to students, to inspire them to achieve higher musical goals.

For more details see: *www.varsityvocals.com*

**ON-LINE COMMUNITY**
The Mainely A CAPPELLA catalog has a popular home page on the World Wide Web, at *www.a–cappella.com*. There are more than 20,000 RealAudio® and MP3 sound clips to hear, an extensive and continually updated concert calendar, and secure on-line buying. There is also a very active newsgroup on the Internet designed exclusively for a cappella fans: *rec.music.a–cappella* (on the web at *groups.google.com* ).

**For more information contact us:**

**PO Box 159**
**Southwest Harbor, ME 04679**
**Phone: 1.800.827.2936**
**International: 1.207.244.7603**
**Fax: 1.207.244.7613**
**Email: catalog@a-cappella.com**
**World Wide Web: www.a-cappella.com**
**For a FREE catalog call: 1.800.827.2936**